About Penguins

For the One who created penguins.
—*Genesis* 1:21

Published by
PEACHTREE PUBLISHERS
1700 Chattahoochee Avenue
Atlanta, Georgia 30318-2112
www.peachtree-online.com

Text © 2009, 2013 by Cathryn P. Sill
Illustrations © 2009, 2013 by John C. Sill

Illustrations created in watercolor on archival quality 100% rag watercolor paper
Text and titles set in Novarese from Adobe Systems

Printed and manufactured in October 2018 by RR Donnelley & Sons in China

10 9 8 7 6 5 4 3 2 (hardcover)
10 9 8 7 6 5 4 3 (trade paperback)
Revised Edition

HC ISBN: 978-1-56145-743-4
PB ISBN: 978-1-56145-741-0

Library of Congress Cataloging-in-Publication Data

Sill, Cathryn P., 1953-
About penguins / written by Cathryn Sill ; illustrated by John Sill.
p. cm.
ISBN 978-1-56145-743-4
1. Penguins—Juvenile literature. I. Sill, John, ill. II. Title.
QL696.S473.S545 2009
598.47—dc22
2008052836

About Penguins

A Guide for Children

Revised Edition

Cathryn Sill

Illustrated by John Sill

Ω

PEACHTREE

ATLANTA

Penguins are seabirds that cannot fly.

They swim very well by using their wings as flippers.

PLATE 2
Fiordland Penguin

Special waterproof feathers keep penguins
warm and dry.

Penguins swim and dive underwater to hunt for food such as fish, squid, and crustaceans.

PLATE 4
Little Penguin

They swim fast and change direction quickly.
This helps them catch food and escape
from predators.

As they swim, some penguins leap from the water and dive back in.

PLATE 6
Gentoo Penguin

Penguins swim slower on the surface of the water.

PLATE 7
Snares Penguin

Penguins move on land by walking, hopping, or sliding.

PLATE 8
Adélie Penguin
Southern Rockhopper Penguin
Emperor Penguin

They come to land to lay eggs and raise chicks.

Penguins may have nests in cold icy areas...

PLATE 10
Emperor Penguin

in wet forests near the ocean…

PLATE 11
Yellow-eyed Penguin

or in hot tropical places.

Some penguins build nests on top of the ground.

PLATE 13
Chinstrap Penguin

Others dig burrows under the ground.

Some penguins build nests in small caves
or cracks in rocks.

Others have no nest. They hold the egg
and then the chick on their feet.

PLATE 16
King Penguin

Penguins work hard to keep their chicks safe.

PLATE 17
Northern Rockhopper Penguin
(*also shown: Brown Skua*)

It is important to protect penguins and
the places where they live.

Afterword

PLATE 1
There are eighteen different kinds of penguins. All of them live in the southern half of the world. They swim in cold ocean currents much of the time. Some penguins spend months at sea. They sleep floating on the ocean. Adélie Penguins have feathers on the base of their bills to warm the air they breathe. They live in cold, icy Antarctica. Climate change seems to be affecting the nesting sites and feeding habits of Adélie Penguins as well as some other species. Scientists are not sure how this will impact the future of these birds.

PLATE 2
The stiff, narrow wings of penguins act like paddles. Penguins use their tails, webbed feet, and flat bills to help them steer as they swim. They almost seem to be flying underwater. Fiordland Penguins spend up to 75 percent of their lives in the ocean. They spend so much time in the water that barnacles often grow on their tails. Fiordland Penguins nest on South Island of New Zealand and on other islands nearby.

PLATE 3
Penguins have short, stiff feathers that grow close together. The feathers overlap to provide protection from water and wind. Penguins waterproof their feathers with oil from a gland at the base of their tails. They spread the oil as they preen (care for) their feathers. In the past, people hunted Royal Penguins and killed them for their oil, which they used in lamps or as fuel. Now that the hunting has ended, their numbers have grown. Royal Penguins live around Macquarie Island in the South Pacific Ocean.

PLATE 4

Penguins have solid, heavy bones that help them dive and swim underwater. Some penguins are able to stay submerged for several minutes before coming to the surface to breathe. Most penguins dive for just a minute or two as they hunt for food. Little Penguins, the smallest kind of penguins, are only around 16 inches (42 cm) tall. They may swim up to 60 miles (95 km) a day looking for food. Little Penguins live around New Zealand and along the southern coast of Australia.

PLATE 5

Penguins must be able to move quickly to catch fast-swimming prey and to escape from predators such as Leopard Seals. Many penguins also swim in large groups for protection from hungry enemies. Macaroni Penguins got their name because of the colorful crests on their heads. They were named after a group of young men from the 1700s called "macaronis" who wore fancy clothes and outlandish hairstyles. Macaroni Penguins live in the South Atlantic and South Indian Oceans.

PLATE 6

Many penguins surge out of the water and dive back in. This form of swimming is called "porpoising." Penguins are able to breathe without slowing down as they porpoise through the water. Moving quickly in and out of the water also replaces the air bubbles under their feathers, which helps keep them warm. Porpoising may help penguins such as Gentoos escape from predators. Gentoo Penguins stay closer to land while hunting. They live in the subantarctic region.

PLATE 7

When swimming on the surface, penguins may be slowed down by waves and water movement. They can use their webbed feet as paddles to propel themselves through the water. While surface swimming, penguins raise their heads—and sometimes their tails—out of the water. Their heavy bodies often stay underwater. Penguins can also bob on the surface, allowing them to rest. On land, Snares Penguins sometimes perch on low branches that are close to their colony. Snares Penguins live around the Snares Islands south of New Zealand.

PLATE 8

Penguins have long claws that grip the ground as they move on land. They walk upright on short, strong legs. Adélie Penguins can walk about as fast as people do. Some penguins hop over ledges and rocks. Rockhopper Penguins are able to climb steep, rocky hillsides. Other kinds of penguins move faster by flopping down and sliding on their bellies. This motion is called "tobogganing." Emperor Penguins sometimes toboggan long distances across the ice to their nesting grounds.

PLATE 9

Almost all penguins nest in colonies. The colonies range in size from just a few nests to thousands of nests. Erect-crested Penguins raise chicks in large colonies on rocky coasts. They nest in colonies on the top of steep slopes on islands south and southeast of New Zealand.

PLATE 10

Emperor Penguins never set foot on land. Large groups of them huddle together on sea ice to stay warm. The father penguins spend all of the cold, dark winter on the frozen ocean taking care of their eggs and chicks. The mothers spend the winter at sea hunting for food. In spring they return to feed and care for the babies. The fathers, who have not eaten for three to four months, return to the ocean to feed themselves. Emperors are the largest penguins. They are 45 inches (115 cm) tall. Only two kinds of penguins (Emperor and Adélie) spend their whole lives in the cold area around Antarctica. There is some concern that warmer temperatures and melting sea ice is threatening Emperor Penguin populations.

PLATE 11

Some penguins build nests among tree roots or under thick bushes. They may line the nests with ferns. Unlike most penguins, Yellow-eyed Penguins do not nest in colonies. They usually build their nests out of sight of their neighbors. They are in danger of becoming extinct. People often destroy their nest sites to create pastureland and farms. Yellow-eyed Penguins live on the southeastern coast of New Zealand and a few islands farther south.

PLATE 12

Galápagos Penguins nest in cracks or crevices among the rocks. Penguins that live in hot places have bare patches of skin on their faces to help them cool down. They may dive into cold water, fluff their feathers out, hold their flippers away from their bodies, or pant to cool themselves. Galápagos Penguins live on the Galápagos Islands at Earth's equator. Warm ocean temperatures caused by El Niño events result in serious shortages of food for Galápagos Penguins.

PLATE 13

Some penguins build nests on the ground to protect their eggs from the cold and to keep them from rolling away. They can use small rocks, parts of plants, mud, or grass. Penguins often squabble over building materials and try to steal pebbles from each other. Chinstrap Penguins build rock nests high enough for protection from flooding caused by melting snow. Chinstraps live on the Antarctic Peninsula and in the subantarctic region.

PLATE 14

Some penguins nest in burrows to protect their eggs and chicks from the hot sun and predators. They use their bills and claws to dig burrows that may be more than 3 feet (90 cm) deep. Magellanic Penguins nest in huge colonies with burrows 3 to 4 feet (90–120 cm) apart. They return to the same burrow year after year. Magellanic Penguins live around the southern part of South America.

PLATE 15

Penguins that live in burrows or in caves often line their nests with grass, twigs, and old feathers. Humboldt Penguins nest in small caves or underground burrows in hot, dry areas along the coasts of Chile and Peru. They swim and hunt in the Humboldt Current, a cold stream of ocean water that flows up from Antarctica.

PLATE 16

Two kinds of penguins (King and Emperor) do not build nests. One of the parents rolls the egg onto its feet. It keeps the egg warm by covering it with a fold of belly skin. If the parent needs to move, it carries the egg with it. King Penguin parents spend over a year nesting and raising a chick. During winter when food is scarce, King chicks may have to go without eating for weeks at a time. King Penguins live in the subantarctic region.

PLATE 17

Most penguins care for their chicks for two to four months. Penguin parents must always be ready to protect their nests. Predators such as Brown Skuas will grab and eat unguarded eggs or chicks. Rockhopper Penguins are quick to attack anything that threatens them. There are two species of Rockhopper Penguins, Northern and Southern. They live in the subantarctic region and on some islands farther north.

PLATE 18

Even though laws around the world protect penguins, these seabirds still face many dangers. Human activities are often a threat to penguin populations. Clearing land for development can destroy penguin habitat. Oil from spills pollutes the water and coats penguins' feathers, causing them to die. Overfishing in some areas makes it hard for penguins to find food. African Penguin numbers have gone down rapidly over the last several years. African Penguins live along the southern coast of Africa.

GLOSSARY

Barnacle—a small saltwater shellfish that attaches itself to an object in the water
Chick—a young bird
Colony—a group of the same kind of animals or plants that live together
Current—a stream of water that flows in the ocean
El Niño—cycles of unusually warm Pacific Ocean temperatures near the equator
Equator—an imaginary line around the middle of the earth halfway between the North and South Poles
Habitat—the place where an animal or plant lives and grows
Predator—an animal that lives by hunting and eating other animals
Prey—an animal that is hunted and eaten by a predator
Species—a group of animals or plants that are alike in many ways
Squid—a sea animal similar to an octopus with ten arms and a tube-shaped body
Subantarctic—near or just above Antarctica

BIBLIOGRAPHY

BOOKS

The Penguin Book: Birds in Suits by Dr. Mark Norman (Black Dog Books)
Penguins by Seymour Simon (Collins)
Penguins! by Wayne Lynch (Firefly Books)
Penguins of the World by Wayne Lynch (Firefly Books)
Welcome to the Whole World of Penguins by Diane Swanson (Whitecap Books)

WEBSITES

http://ibc.lynxeds.com/family/penguins-spheniscidae
http://kids.nationalgeographic.com/Animals/
http://www.adelie.pwp.blueyonder.co.uk/
http://www.kidzone.ws/animals/penguins/index.htm
http://www.seaworld.org/animal-info/info-books/penguin/appendix-species.htm

ABOUT... SERIES

HC: 978-1-68263-031-0
PB: 978-1-68263-032-7

HC: 978-1-56145-038-1
PB: 978-1-56145-364-1

HC: 978-1-56145-688-8
PB: 978-1-56145-699-4

HC: 978-1-56145-301-6
PB: 978-1-56145-405-1

HC: 978-1-56145-987-2
PB: 978-1-56145-988-9

HC: 978-1-56145-588-1
PB: 978-1-56145-837-0

HC: 978-1-56145-881-3
PB: 978-1-56145-882-0

HC: 978-1-56145-757-1
PB: 978-1-56145-758-8

HC: 978-1-56145-906-3

HC: 978-1-56145-358-0
PB: 978-1-56145-407-5

PB: 978-1-56145-406-8

HC: 978-1-56145-795-3

HC: 978-1-56145-743-4
PB: 978-1-56145-741-0

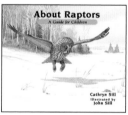
HC: 978-1-56145-536-2
PB: 978-1-56145-811-0

HC: 978-1-56145-907-0
PB: 978-1-56145-908-7

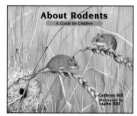
HC: 978-1-56145-454-9
PB: 978-1-56145-914-8

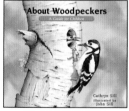
HC: 978-1-68263-004-4

ALSO AVAILABLE IN SPANISH AND BILINGUAL EDITIONS
• About Amphibians / Sobre los anfibios / 978-1-68263-033-4 PB • About Birds / Sobre los pájaros / 978-1-56145-783-0 PB • Sobre los pájaros / 978-1-68263-071-6 PB
• About Fish / Sobre los peces / 978-1-56145-989-6 PB • About Insects / Sobre los insectos / 978-1-56145-883-7 PB • About Mammals / Sobre los mamíferos / 978-1-56145-800-4 PB • Sobre los mamíferos / 978-1-68263-072-3 PB • About Reptiles / Sobre los reptiles / 978-1-56145-909-4 PB

ABOUT HABITATS SERIES

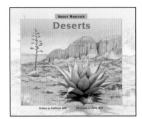
Deserts

HC: 978-1-56145-641-3
PB: 978-1-56145-636-9

Forests

HC: 978-1-56145-734-2

Grasslands

HC: 978-1-56145-559-1
PB: 978-1-68263-034-1

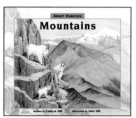
Mountains

HC: 978-1-56145-469-3
PB: 978-1-56145-731-1

Oceans

HC: 978-1-56145-618-5
PB: 978-1-56145-960-5

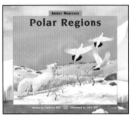
Polar Regions

HC: 978-1-56145-832-5

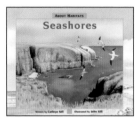
Seashores

HC: 978-1-56145-968-1

Wetlands

HC: 978-1-56145-432-7
PB: 978-1-56145-689-5

THE SILLS

Cathryn Sill, a former elementary school teacher, is the author of the acclaimed ABOUT... series. With her husband John and her brother-in-law Ben Sill, she coauthored the popular bird-guide parodies, A FIELD GUIDE TO LITTLE-KNOWN AND SELDOM-SEEN BIRDS OF NORTH AMERICA, ANOTHER FIELD GUIDE TO LITTLE-KNOWN AND SELDOM-SEEN BIRDS OF NORTH AMERICA, and BEYOND BIRDWATCHING.

John Sill is a prize-winning and widely published wildlife artist who illustrated the ABOUT... series and illustrated and coauthored the FIELD GUIDES and BEYOND BIRDWATCHING. A native of North Carolina, he holds a B.S. in Wildlife Biology from North Carolina State University.

The Sills live in Franklin, North Carolina.